Suzanne & Louise Kelman's

Big Purple Undies

To Countess Ardoll
Keep laughing
at life
Suzanne Kel

Inhoa Publishing
Promoting Positive Publications
ABN 87 523 594 805

First published in Australia in 2003
Inhoa Publishing
ABN 87 523 594 805

For information regarding permissions write to:
Inhoa Publishing
PO Box 3229 Joondalup WA 6027
Telephone: (08) 9401 2678 Fax (08) 9401 5922
Website: www.inhoa.com

Attention: Permissions- S&L Kelman
Visit our website: www.bigpurpleundies.com

ISBN 0-9580869-6-6

Printed in Australia by The Printing Factory

Acknowledgments

To all our families and friends.
With special thanks to

My husband, Nigel- Wearer of the "Purple Undies" and to my daughter,
Molly who likes to put them on her head.
Penny Baker- Illustrator Extraordinaire

My husband, Matthew who wouldn't be seen dead in Purple Undies, and
my son, Christopher who I'd like to keep undies on.
Suzanne Kelman- The Kooky Kansas Crackpot

My Husband, Michael who refuses to wear undies and my children, Jonah
and Ellie who constantly remind him he should.
Louis Kelman - The Biggest and Best

My husband, John who's glad I don't write about his undies and my
daughter, Odette who wishes I would.
*Jane Dowling- Anything but Plain Editor (No it's not spelled @ *!!*) who
could even cope with our spelling.*

With thanks to God for the great sense of humour He gave us and his unfailing love.

Contents

Big Purple Undies

How come I'm still single at 40 Lord
When I've done everything that I could?
I've prayed and believed. I've cried and received,
By all of Your promises stood.

I've hung a big pair of purple undies
on the end of the bedpost at night,
to help me believe You could indeed
fill them with a cute Mr Right.

But, Lord, they're starting to look shabby.
The stitching's coming apart at the seam.
The cat has started to claw them.
And my nephew thinks they're a scream.

I've looked 'round the church for a wearer
to put them on and be mine.
So far, Lord, there are no takers,
And any two legs will do fine.

I don't mind if he's a bit saggy,
Bald as a coot, and jiggles a lot
I'm really not fussy about worn 'round the edges
as Bridget Bardot I am not!

I just want someone to put on my old purple undies
and dance 'round not caring a jot...
Then throw off those old purple undies
and love me with all that he's got!

Wonder Woman I Ain't

I've kicked off my glittery boots
As wonder woman I ain't.
Thrown off that curly black wig
And the crown with flaking gold paint.

I've settled myself in the bath,
And draped my head in the water.
It seems yesterday I was a child
Jumping skip rope; somebody's daughter.

A gush of wind, I was a wife;
A bountiful, beautiful bride
With a strong and handsome husband
The future was open wide.

Then I became someone's mother.
Instant Motherhood; straight off the racks
But where has Me gone?
I think I slipped down one of the cracks.

What happened to my get up and go?
And "Life is what you make it."
It's turned into "Take a warm sweater."
And "It's cheaper to stay home and bake it!"

I really haven't got a lot to complain about
My family is healthy and happy.
The children are growing so fast,
And it's the last I've seen of a nappy.

I've just changed into somebody else
As I stare at my own reflection
I'm not asking for fame and fortune
White teeth or body perfection.

Who am I? Where am I going?
It's a fair question to ask
On this my life journey.
What is my mission, my task?

That's when I hear a quiet voice
His soft and beautiful tone,
"Love me with all of your heart,
And love each one as your own."

"Give Me all of your worries.
Cast them all upon Me
Look up to heaven and count your blessings.
It'll all come good, you'll see."

There's Nothing Like a Piece of Chocolate

There's nothing like a piece of chocolate
when your washing's gone pink or grey.
I watch it blowing in the wind
like a firework gone astray.

It's that smooth and creamy taste
that slips with ease down within.
I keep it in a very secret place
And hide the wrappers in the bin.

It's such a wonderful, confident feeling
as you undo that shiny new wrapper.
Oh, what wonder awaits you
That instant feel-good zapper.

It's my only real vice.
That, and potato chips.
Oh, to the man who invented chocolate -
I'd like to kiss you smack on the lips!

The Hormone Patch

This patch is doing wonders for my hormones,
At night I simply stick it on my tum.
One morning I was frantically searching,
Then I saw it there, stuck on his bum.

Gently I tried to peel and not disturb him
But firmly it was stuck and he awoke
He jumped up late for work and started dressing
Unaware of my own private joke.

He was cranky; being late made him angry.
He snapped when I offered him food.
The door slammed, as I sat in my nightie,
And wondered if the patch would help his mood.

All day I couldn't help but giggle
As I thought of the patch in its place.
If only they could see through pinstripe,
That would sure put a smile on each face.

As his car pulled into the driveway I was eager
to see how his day had turned out.
But instead of his usual greeting
he started kicking his briefcase about.

He ranted his day had been awful!
And he thought he must have the 'flu.
In the office he'd had twenty seven hot flushes,
and tearfully ran to the loo.

His voice seemed a slight octave higher
as I sympathetically felt his head.
He announced to us all he had a migraine
And in my slippers he flounced off to bed.

That night I removed the offending item.
I told the kids no longer to hide
Tomorrow Dad would be back to normal
He'd just been in touch with his feminine side.

What Have You Done Today, Love?

"What have you done today, love?"
The same thing he asks me each day,
As I come out from under the table
My hair on end, my face grey.

Should I start with the bum wipes and nappies?
Or the chocolate pudding thrown up the door?
Or maybe the Great Shopping Tantrum
As the little darlings lay rigid on the floor.

Should I mention the half hour showdown
As I wrestled one into a carseat
Or the icecreams they threw from the stroller
That landed on somebody's feet?

At the library they'd thrown a big wobbly
And screaming, they'd run down the aisle,
With livid librarians chasing them
They didn't stop for a mile.

Should I show him my lunch sandwich,
half-eaten, still on the plate
As I'd run to save the cat from the toilet
Where they'd dangled him screeching his fate.

Should I tell I've had no adult conversation
since he'd left for work this morn?
Although I've sung "Baa Baa Black Sheep"
Till my throat was dry and worn.

About the twenty minutes I'd been sobbing
When they'd gone and I'd looked everywhere.
And turned the house upside down searching
When I heard, "BOO!" from under a chair.

When - sweet relief- their eyelids gently closed,
they'd snored and they'd napped.
Comatosed I lay on the sofa
Every strength in my body zapped.

"What have I done today, love?
Glad you asked. I'll sum it up for you.
It's a good thing I do this job for love
'Cause you'd owe me a million or two."

When a Mother Leaves Home Forever

When a mother leaves home forever
it will be at exactly quarter past six,
with her dinner bubbling and boiling,
kids screaming, the dog being sick.

Pulling off her rubber gloves and apron,
Kicking dirty washing into the air,
she'll pack her two outfits- her wardrobe-
in a black plastic bag with no care.

She'll hand her husband her To Do List;
each child she'll kiss on the head,
and out of the door with a flurry
to a life of freedom instead.

She'll walk to the first travel agent,
book a flight to anywhere hot,
where cabana boys can serve her
all the good food that they've got.

She'll think of her young offspring often,
and maybe she'll shed a tear,
then off to the disco to dance
in her new non-childproof leather gear.

She'll sit up all night for the sunrise
as there's no school or homework to do.
She'll run into the waves screaming wildly
and anything else inappropriate too!
She'll write letters and listen to music.

When she feels like it she'll go on a hike.
Or sit on a rock all day singing.
Or take off on her new Harley bike.

She looks at the flour and sugar
her dreams lost again in the mix.
Maybe tomorrow she'll leave home forever...
And go exactly at quarter past six.

Dancing Dentures

My husband ran off with a bimbo,
"A mid-life crisis!" everyone said.
But I really missed having a fella,
there seemed such a big hole in my bed.

I looked at myself in the mirror.
Middle aged, plump, with false teeth.
Who on earth could I be kidding?
Too old to turn over a new leaf!

Then I saw a sign on a lamppost
On Saturday- A planned Singles night.
If I could just muster up courage
at the end of my tunnel was light.

So I took myself off to the hairdressers,
and they bleached, they permed and they trimmed.
New make-up and outfit were bought then
With a girdle my tummy was thinned.

I arrived that night feeling fantastic.
Tottering in heels; a goddess galore.
First went to the bar for dutch courage.
On the stool next to me sat the Town Bore.

He talked me to death all the evening.
Though I tried, I couldn't get away
to check out the talent on the dance floor-
listening to his joke on that stool did I stay.

As the music droned on I grew tired
And I couldn't help stifling a yawn.
As a joke he stuck in his fat finger
and from my gums my dentures were torn.

They flew up in the air like a rocket
"We have lift-off!" NASA would say.
All I could do is watch in sheer horror
as my choppers were flying away.

They headed on course for the dance floor
ricocheting down off the disco ball,
straight down the collar of a cutie,
jiggling alone, so handsome, so tall.

Hot and flustered I raced to his side there
heart pounding, in my throat a large lump
and careful not to flash him a smile
asked to join him in dancing The Bump.

He looked shocked and a little excited
to be propositioned in such a direct way,
but with gusto we started dancing
as the music started to play.

I kept trying to feel for my dentures
As I groped each wrinkle and fold.
With a wry smile he made a comment
how he liked his women so bold.

He pulled me in close for a slow dance;
a conquering smile at the prize he had got
but his body visibly stiffened
as up the back of his shirt my hand shot.

Up by his left armpit I found them
and though I tried they were just out of reach.
Then they slipped down the back of his trousers
and he yelled as they bit his left cheek!

We got married a year ago Christmas
but there was no bride on top of our cake.
We just thought it was terribly fitting
to have some dentures entwining her mate.

Remember !! A hundred belly laughs is as

good as fifteen minutes on the treadmill

I Wish Carol Would Step Down From The Choir

I do wish Carol would step down from the choir, Lord
and start serving tea and biscuits instead
'cause if her high C gets any higher
I think we'll see Mr Jones back from the dead!

She stands right in front of the pulpit,
A shock of red hair and white teeth,
Jiggling, clapping, and singing…
Puts me right off my Sunday roast beef!

Oh Lord, I know she's the body.
And I should love her all of the time.
But if there's any justice in Heaven
Surely murdering "Amazing Grace" is a crime.

Last week she started a stomping
The floorboards could not take her lot.
Bouncing Mrs Brown right off her piano stool -
into the arms of the vicar she shot!

Maybe You could have a word, Lord
as we've tried to tactfully tell her she's bad.
We'd encourage her in another gifting
if we could only think of one that she had.

Maybe she's not singing as much for Your glory,
As she stands there bold and tall,
Reminding us that loving everybody
is the most important commandment of all.

Hanging Out The Washing

I used to think washing was a chore
Till I discovered my imagination.
As I hung out the vest and pants
I'm transported to a far-off location.

Riding on elephant back
in a dark and rugged terrain.
Flower in clenched teeth, dancing
with a cute matador in Spain.

I'm sipping tea with the Queen
And I give her some family advice.
(On goes another shirt)
"More tea or cucumber slice?"

I love the pyramids this time of year...
(On goes the last pair of shorts.)
Yes, the cruise has been marvellous,
we stopped in all kinds of ports.

Oh, blast! I've run out of pegs,
And just when it was getting fun...
I was married to a famous gangster
Being chased; life on the run.

Let's put on another load.
I've got plenty more places to see.
And you thought washing was boring.
A sprinkle of imagination, you'll see...

How I Wish There Was An Ironing Fairy

How I wish there was an ironing fairy,
Who appeared when given the sign
Like the basket spilling over
And the voices starting to whine.

Mom, is my blue shirt ironed?
Those trousers could sure use a pleat.
He starts to iron like crazy,
with vigour he turns up the heat.

Yes, the fairy would indeed be a male
Dressed in a full tutu with glitters and stars
As I'm stretching out watching "Oprah"
he'd be ironing my knickers and bras

He's finished and he's worked like crazy,
You can hardly see him for steam.
When suddenly I awake from my slumber
and realise it's all been a dream...

The Spammogram

I opened the door to the clinic,
gave my name and waited in fear.
The nurse's shadow was like the Grim Reaper.
The moment I dreaded was here.

She shouted my name like a drill sergeant,
I followed behind like a lamb.
I knew that the machine was waiting
to turn my boobs into spam.

She boomed out the General Procedure.
I stripped to my waist as was told.
She took hold of my breast like fresh mincemeat
and slapped it into the mould.

She pushed a whole lot of buttons
grinning coldly from where she was sat
saying, "This won't hurt a bit, dear"
as the machine came down with a Splat!

I kept my lips tightly sealed.
The pain in my breast was ablaze.
As pummeling and squeezing continued
the rest went into a haze.

At last the torture was over.
I peeled myself off the bar.
She rolled my breasts up like two cocktail sausages
and dropped them into my bra.

Stunned, I went to the waiting room,
visions dancing away in my mind-
of finding the machine's inventor
seeing him and his machine intertwined.

Then I'd slam it down on his Manhood
with a thundering splat and a thud,
asking his wife if she preferred better
her all-new flat-packed stud.

"Can I get you something for the pain, dear?"
said the receptionist with a smug grin.
I said, "Have you got two sesame seed buns
to put these two hamburgers in?"

She looked at me half-amused
as I paid without making a fuss.
Then grabbing hold of my composure
I made my way to the bus.

The bus driver was rather chatty,
he said his name was Sam.
Asked what I was cooking for dinner,
I said, "Well, I know it won't be spam!"

It's Sunday School Again, Dear Jesus
(Give Me All of the Grace that You've Got!)

It's Sunday school again, dear Jesus
Give me all of the grace that you've got.
I know I shouldn't be scared , Lord,
But my stomach's tied up in a knot.

When I took on this role with such meaning,
"A Ministry for God," I was told.
They just happened to neglect to tell me
The last teacher was carried out cold!

One sweet little six year old named David
Fired a slingshot while heads bowed and prayed,
Maybe he thought he was getting Goliath
but that was no giant he slayed!

Last week there was such a ruckus,
Daniel got a finger stuck in an ear,
It was peanut butter that was the culprit
and the victim was sweet little Leah.

Then at 10:55 precisely,
To the toilet they all had to go
There was water, paper and soap, Lord
covering the walls high and low.

We handed out the snacks, Lord.
I don't know how Jenny's got into her eyes.
And Ryan crept in the cupboard
Filling his pockets with extra supplies.

I asked if anyone in the class knew Jesus
and a sweet little thing with blonde hair
Said: "Does he work up the road in the chip shop?
'Cause I like the pies they serve there."

We stood in a ring to say prayers, Lord
And I asked them if they had a request,
But when Tim shared his dad's little problem
I blushed right the way down to my vest.

It was while we sang "We Love You, Lord"
at the back Carol started to cry
'Cause Peter had got hold of her dolly
and launched it right into the sky

So I ask you, dear Lord, to help me.
Who knows what today's going to be?
You said let the children come to You, Lord.
Maybe today you could take them for me!

Do That Hokey-Pokey Dance Again, Mom

Do the hokey-pokey dance again, Mom
And wear the flowery tea cosy on your head.
Get out your platform shoes, Mom
and Bay City Rollers shorts in tartan red.

Show us once again those crazy pictures
when all your boyfriends had an afro-hairdo.
Remind us when you were the dancing queen, Mom
and flick your hips like John Travolta too.

Tell us how you were really groovy.
Paint your eyes in green and powder blue.
get out all your funky jewellery, Mom.
And kiss your Donny Osmond poster too.

Dust off that strange Rubik's Cube, Mom.
Let's play with that old Pac-Man game.
Sing along again to Donna Summer, Mom.
And tell us how today's music ain't the same.

Remind us, Mom, about your brother's Chopper,
and how you sang along to "Grease" that summer back.
Get out your David Cassidy pin, Mom.
And let us try on your crazy fur-lined mack.

I do hope when I'm as old as you are, Mom
I will do this hokey-pokey dance like you
And wear a flowery tea cosy on my head, Mom
And remember the crazy things TODAY we do!

In A Hundred Years Time

In a hundred years time it won't matter
If the house you've lived in wasn't done,
the garden and outside wasn't finished,
or the chores not begun.

In a hundred years time it won't matter
if the paint still sat in the tin,
that was meant for the wall in the study.
Would it really be such a sin?

In a hundred years time it won't matter
if that shiny new car was not yours?
Or that fancy new watch you'd admired
still sat in the case at the stores?

In a hundred years it won't matter
If you were never on TV,
You'd never reached Hollywood stardom
Or even been in a movie.

At sunset a graveyard is quiet
As you quietly move through the leaves
You'll see life summed up on each headstone.
What kind of treasures are these?

Store up your treasures in heaven
where thieves and moths cannot find.
Love God, love your neighbour as yourself
be patient, gentle, and kind.

Live today and enjoy it.
Grasp every moment you can.
For Life is the eternal race-
No winners, it's just that you ran.

"Big Purple Undies"
To Help you with our Lingo
Translation Guide

ENGLISH	AMERICAN	AUSTRALIAN
Y- Fronts	Tidy- whities	Undies
Nappy	Diaper	Nappy
Rubbish bin	Trash can	Bin
Wet Wipes	Wet Ones	Bum Wipes
Wobbly	Tantrum	Stinky
Toilet / Loo	Bathroom / Potty	Dunny
Biscuits	Cookies	Bikkies
Vicar	Pastor	Minister
Wash Line	Laundry Line / Tumbledryer	Hills Hoist
Fella	Guy	Bloke
Town Bore	The man your Mom wanted you to marry	Drongo
Chips	Fries	Chips
Vest	Undershirt	Singlet
Tea cosy	Tea pot warmer	Tea cosy
Mincemeat	Hamburger	Mince